Unsweet Dreams

ANNE LE MARQUAND HARTIGAN

*When is passion
Out of fashion?*

salmonpoetry

Published in 2011 by
Salmon Poetry
Cliffs of Moher, County Clare, Ireland
Website: www.salmonpoetry.com
Email: info@salmonpoetry.com

ISBN 978-1-907056-86-4

COVER ARTWORK: *Anne Le Marquand Hartigan*
COVER DESIGN: *Siobhán Hutson*

PRINTED IN IRELAND

*Salmon Poetry receives financial support from
The Arts Council / An Chomhairle Ealaíon*

For my grandchildren:

Diarmuid, Florence, Colm, Elizabeth, Inis, Patrick, Zoe, Cherri, Naoise, Ruaidhri, Euan, Freya, Garry, Sadhbh, Iona, Dominic, Rosanna, Taig, and granddaughter-in-law Andrea.

Acknowledgements

Thanks are due to the editors of the following where some of these poems appeared:

"Neighbourhood Watch", first appeared in *Something Beginning with P*, editor Seamus Cashman (O'Brien Press, 2004).

"Heirloom", "If", "Once Upon a Time" and "Dark Goddess" from *Long Tongue* (Beaver Row Press, Dublin, 1982).

"Heirloom" first appeared in *Ireland's Other Poetry, Anonymous to Zozimus*, edited by John Wyse Jackson and Hector Mc Donnell (Lilliput Press, 2007). It also appeared on *Poems on the Underground* (The Poetry Society, London).

"Eve" from *Immortal Sins* (Salmon Poetry, 1995).

"Forgive Us Our Trespasses" first appeared in *The Clifden Anthology* 2007, edited by Brendan Flynn.

"Unsweet Dreams" from *Nourishment* by Anne Le Marquand Hartigan (Salmon Poetry, 2005).

"Viewing the Landscape" then titled "In Praise of Objectivity" first appeared in *Southword* (2002), edited by Patrick Galvin.

"Moon" was published in *The Irish Times* in 2010.

Set aside delay and thought of gain
and mindful of darkness burning mix
brief sottisness with wisdom while you may:
it is sweet to play the clown upon occasion.

From Horace, last verse of Ode number 12
"Iam veris comites" *Odes, Book 1V*

Contents

PART ONE – Rhyming Cutlets
Shorter Poems

PART TWO

PART THREE

PART ONE

Rhyming Cutlets

Shorter Poems

Heirloom

My father said,
It's always
Good weather
In bed.

Eve

She sat on the lip
of events

waiting

for some new mouth
to open

offering

an original sin

The Two Cs

Women's independence

The car and
The condom

Domestic Economy

The spider is a friendly beast
She doesn't worry in the least
So when she wants a bite or sup
She gaily eats her husband up.

"It Ain't What You Do It's The Way That You Do It..."

Tiny flies
Tiny bugs

Who land on my summer book

Bigger than a flea
But not much

There you are
In vast ecstasy,

You copulate
On my page's
White strand

As one you land
As one you take the air,

What does it feel like fly
Making love up there ?

The Sheets

The simple things are lovely
The simple things are free
To lie with my arms about you
When you slip into bed with me.

Wine of Life

Sweetheart! All this time apart
in space, a make, a waste, a start

that all begins and edges on
in our strange live continuum,

our sweet song, untitled dumb
breaking bounds and rules of thumb

has no place in daily time
to burst, to rush, all out of line

our stream is fresh it breaks the banks
I raise this song and give my thanks.

Fancier

Come little pigeon
Take a message to my love,
Say what I dare not

On your pink leg
Carry my heart.

Fulfil

If you were a jug

Round, fat,
Comfortable

I would fill you
To the brim

Then, dive in.

Marriage

We expect heaven

We are given

Earth.

A Joker

Juggling
with his despair

Pitching globes
of laughter

to the air.

Bedsong

In a Guest House

Someone woke me in the night
a little cry
two small cries;

then the bedsprings
up and down
down and up

the bedsprings

creak ting
crawk ping
bedsprings singing.

Line Engaged

If you write
love poems
at the end
of a telephone book

Oh la la etc

I think you should
tear the page out

otherwise
give her a ring,

La oh oh etc

I know that's
a terrible pun, but

what would
you expect
from a telephone
book's bottom?

Fear of the Dark

for a moment
one summer night
we lifted each other
into the light.

Gift of Sight

Cup your hand
protect protect the flame
do not let the candle out
you may not
see again.

A Knot in Her Handkerchief

Never will I forget

Says she

Struggling to remember...

Relationship

They eat
each other
minced.

Each day
the elder
turns the handle.

The younger
pours in
her guts.

Radha

This man has had many women
Swift sorties on sofas, in bars,
Always hoping he will find his Radha
Always hoping he will not find her.

The Cutting Edge

Not only the knife
  Takes life

A word's sharp dart
  Flays the heart

Shoot Out

Words are bullets
lying in their sheaths
resting, polished, alert
for deadly deeds.

Immortality

Dogs' souls
are just the same
as ours

non-existent

The Address Book

I have had Enough.

A line though your name
A straight line firm and hard.
I've dropped you.

You'll bounce.

Postscript

Watching telly is 'till death
My Brother

Reflection

Oh the weary place
That is my face.

Bodywise

Taking pleasure   the body

loves to give its graces
hot kisses, warmth
from our depths   life so
short so brief – body

gives such sweet relief
from the day to day
sweat and toil –
but in the end

we all meet in the soil.

PART TWO

Unsweet Dreams

Because of coffee
taken late
I meet the morning
early

I lie here
without a mate
straight haired
or curly

is this how
we meet our fate
out of step
and churly

catch a breath
in such a state
toss and turn

ourselves berate
in a sweat
and surly?

With life or death
we have a date
never falling
fairly

'tis sleep I want
at any rate
landing on me
squarely

dreams to come
and tuck me up
call me sweet
and dearie

but night it just
hammers on
the moon slides by
so pearly

full and round
complete it is
staring at me
surely

underneath its
chilling beams
the mind goes round
so whirly

if I sleep now
I'll wake up late
oh God I'm in
a shocking state

perhaps I'd better
masturbate
forget about the
heaven's gate,

oh morning
will you never come
and send the sun
to shine upon
this girly?

Who's lost all hope
does toss and curse
this night has been
the blasted worst

and as I reach the
final verse I've bills
to pay, my zip has burst
I've put on weight
that's not the worst

oh where is love
give me a break
pale morning creeps
its place to take
in shattered sleep
a head that aches
this life is all a
bloody fake and just
you note the big mistake
to live a life
let them eat cake −

Because of coffee
taken late
I greet this morning
         early.

Carbon Dating

Is love out of date?
Who wears it ?

Is it fashionable?
I can't see it around.

Must be lying
in some attic

dusted occasionally –
a sort of antique.

Could we get a
few quid for it?

Love, so innocent
and troublesome,

we will never
suffer it,

it can behave
in an ugly fashion.

Wouldn't have it
near you

if I were you.
Doesn't pay.

There are no
Bonuses or discounts.

No one does it
nowadays

wouldn't dream
of such un-cool behaviour.

We are all PC
in control.

Keep in top form
with exercise

foreign holidays – and
regular sex –

for the health.

Rock Rock Rock-a-bye Baby

Sex is just so good for you
it cheers you up at night,

If you know all the positions
and learn to do it right,

Soothing when you're sober
giggly when you're tight

It can keep you healthy
when you learn to do it right.

Oh lovely sweet and
playful sex you are my

Dear delight you link
my spirit and my soul

So make my body light
after we've said our

Goodnight prayers
turned down the light

My body dispels
its lingering fears

When held
so close and tight – oh

Sex is just so good for us
it cheers us up at night

When we know all the positions
and learn to do it right.

Soothing when we're sober
giggly when we're tight

It is so much fun for us
When we make love all the night.

A Toast

Do what you do do well girl!
Do what you do do well

Make a good meal
Have a good laugh

Raise a full glass
To a happy fuck

Let all literary
Aspirations go to hell –

So many
Tossed in the muck

The No's can nod and nod
Taking life to pieces bit by bit

An intelligent jigsaw?
Where do I fit ?

Nowhere – so – why bother
Down a glass and love!
My brother.

Once Upon a Time

I do not know what it means to you,
But I must plan
What I'm going to do when I am dead.
After all it might happen anytime,
You should plan ahead.

There is a time for everything
And everything has its accorded place

I can only live my allotted span, and
If it catches me when I am unaware
If it catches me before I've said my prayers,
Made my will had my fill of life

Just because I have so much to do
So much to say
So many strings untied
So many things untried...

We have one life or two?

And always as you know I must
Get those curtains washed and dried
And that picture sitting on the floor
I must hang it up upon the wall.
All that I have said or left unsaid...

I worry sometimes
That Peter will be there after all
With all those goats and sheep
Will they all be shitting on the floor?
Will I be asked to enter through the door?

Have I loved the poor?

My sins will sit in dustbins at my side
What sins will pour down upon my head?

I might as well be dead

But time, time, time,
Time and again
All that time
What will we do?

Sit knitting
Fitting small space
Into smaller space?
Intricate eternal lace?

When I am dead will I see your face?

Will I be offered a sweetened cup of tea?
A pill of memory? A peace of mind?

What is there for me to find
Can I plan ahead?
Can I fit this jigsaw into place?
Is this the only piece of time we get,
Now, with piles and falling hair and splitting ends,
Bags under the eyes,
Those brown envelopes they send?

The things that I have left undone,
Those things that I will never do.
Those loves that I have left unsung,
Each second ticking I have more to do
Each morning freshening is a wasted day.
Others here have done it all before.

I have seen the dead,
Seen the body stiffen, the jaw hang
The body shrink and tighten as the spirit fled

The known face become unknowable.

My brains are pounding out the normal pain,
The cut finger on the sardine tin,
The struggle constantly to get thin

I should have time

Time for this and that
Where to find the pattern
Where the tune
Where the knowledge

Have you fed the cat?

You would think you could take care of that.
Can I take this medicine on a spoon
Can I wash this stain out of my dress?
Fill the gap up with a safety pin?

Oh those kisses,
Kisses, kisses,
Bathed in sweat
Between our breasts.

The letters lie unopened
The bill unpaid,
The account unsettled,
The dear sirs unless…

O the Dear Sirs…

Bathed in sweat
Between our thighs
Between our eyes

Nevertheless…

Can you do a cartwheel on the sand
Send the world a-spinning round your head
Can you see the stars between your feet?
The jellyfish are jumping round the bed

This baloney
This ballyhoo
Nevertheless

At this particular moment in time,
Take time, mark and for the time being,
May I stress
It gives me great pleasure
To open this Bazaar,
This Fête

Worse than Death.

Untrue: That's You

Thank you for your
untrue love

So constant, singular
like flu

Always there when
I don't want

Never around to prove
you're true — oh

untrue love don't
let you down

Untrue love has every
hue   to colour

All the stars above
Wrecking, wounding

Making blue all
the sunny skies I love.

Untrue love I know
you well   how

You never fail to stew
things into a jolly pulp

Untrue love does not
turn up — the phone

Forgets to ring
for you, always late

Forgets the date of
birthdays – Christmases

I'm telling you – You can
count on Untrue Love

It will never fail
to do   all the things

That piss you off
why can't I say

THAT'S IT
I'M THROUGH

PS

So when the earth falls
on your grave

I will not cry boo-hoo for you
Oh NO boo hoo for you,

That's a thing I will not do
Not one little boo hoo for you.

Song to the Unfaithful

Remember O man
To your last dying day
What you destroyed
What games you played.

The lies you told
With clear open eye
Used good to cheat
To cause me die.

To your last dying day
May your heart weigh lead
The curse of a woman
Can dis-ease your bed

Seep into your bowels
Your eyes, your spleen
Into your soul
Make grey dead your dream,

Remember O Man
To your last dying day
What you destroyed,
What you tore away.

A Pocket Full of Rye

Will I ever love again
as I loved you with all I had?
Will I ever trust and spend
my life my blood my soul myself?

I simply loved you as a breath
as one I could not live without,
as one whose pulse beat with mine,
as one whose mind lay in my brain.

When death reaches out a hand
to take my soul out of my flesh,
to lay it in eternity, will you
be there to share my rest?

Will it be rest, or just a void
a nothing   a space   an emptiness?
None of us can know or warn
and none of us can have redress.

I would wish to love anew,
give this world a kiss of life,
it was you that turned your back,
it was your hand that held the knife.

PART THREE

Not a Word

Don't say a word…

*Poem written on a sick bag on a flight
between Dublin and Heathrow*

I stuffed the words down carefully
though they protested; said
they were made for better things

I held the bag quite shut
and shook them up. They
did not like that.

Shut your eyes I said
and you will be in for
a Big Surprise.

They grumbled a bit, but
did as they were told
(for once) they knew

Something was up.
I think they hoped
they would become

A mistresspiece.
The good word –
oh immortality!

Sssh, says I, we're
going through Customs
and words can be considered

dangerous
in a poet's hands.
You might be banned!

Oh they were quiet,
they shivered.
What paltry things…

Sweet creatures. Says I
here's your surprise, count
to three, then open all

Your little eyes and see!
I plopped them in the litter bin.
They had no guts.

I didn't wait to hear
their squeaks. But
sauntered to the exit

Word and duty free…

Not all words please.

Viewing the Landscape

Either the subject or the object, women
are useful to decorate a frieze or lie in a poem
black skinned or white whichever increases the tension
the sensuousness, the sexuality of the pose or picture.

We rest in the landscape, are the hills and valleys
oh, how un-nice, our cleft and cleavage and holes etc. –
we are useful to walk on or over or through, or to appear
– unspoilt native sort of thing – shyly, timidly in doorways
in the half light and mostly – waiting

waiting for something to happen
waiting for someone else to make the waves.

Ah of course, we too *are* the sea moaning and
sighing for loss and deprivation, groaning for the man
who has gone, or *we* drowned him… Nasty schemers
murderous women, ball crushers etc., that we are.

So there we are on a cold sea shore,
black shawl held around a white face – a place
none of us would wait in for a minute –
but buzz home in the Porsche – turn on the telly

And pour a neat whiskey

Heart Transplant

Throughout the drag of history
   Women have been privileged
To change their minds.

Standing in doubtful liberty
   I find with some timidity
I have changed mine.

Now rightly I should be able
   To lay my cards upon the table
Like a man.

But history has defeated me
   I have no freedom – what is free?
My shackled tongue

I would say yes where I said no
   But I do blush to tell you so
O give me calm.

For I do wish to lie with thee
   So let a happy loving be
And place no bind

A giving – free and kind.

Goodbye for Now Computer

As this little silver pen
slides to write my wobble
          now again

Santa brought you to me
in the night silent and shiny
          giving bright

thought a way to move along
in line – linking my words across
          the turd of time

I trust your marks. Imperfect
scribbler me – my blessings on you pen
          I am set free.

Drawing The Line

Take this line
it holds the soul

makes the mark
along the white

the spirit takes
this swinging flow

to hold and grow
a slice of life

           can we leave
           a mark or sign

           of living life
           in just a line?

Undertow

The mote in the eye

Women have to write
without being drunk,

to fall in the gutter
not for us. Let us take

each word we utter and fling
it far away from couch

silk, satin, linen,
bodice, all the feminine attire,

word must hold a tighter
tension – words of ours

must be
barbed wire.

Be hail, be stone
be juice, be blood,

were not bodies
made from mud?

We swim in the counter stream
underneath we dodge the beam

the mote is ours
by which we see,

blinded is
our liberty?

Forgive Us Our Trespasses

What place do your children give you?

They will allow you to trespass on their
green gardens but wait for you to go
because they tell their friends their secrets
Not you.

You are the beginning for them and they want
you behind but left there. Doing nothing
in particular but not rocking the boat.
Don't do

Anything outrageous until they are middle-aged
then they won't mind because it will reflect well
to have an interesting foremother. Basically it's a
No go area

Parents are increasingly obsolete, dumb dinosaurs
Made to be stuffed

Dark Goddess

It is maytime and my black bitch
Is on heat. Her many suitors
Old, pure bred, or shaggy
Throng the doorstep

Making their music with the blackbird.
Warbling whines and much leg cocking
Meeting her sometimes nose to nose tip
Through the glass door. She growls,

Spliced between the desire and territory,
"O Prisoner of Love"
I, the wicked stepmother
Keep constant guard

Hardhearted to her wistful eyes
Her whimpers and placating tail
I whisk her to the car with well aimed boot
Towards the lovelorn there.

It will soon pass poor girl ,
And they so constant now will flit
Towards mature attractions,
Dustbins; "O fickle Love".

Black Goddess, so soon to be dethroned
Your heady incense
Moonlike is on the wane,
And when out walking

Down the street again
You and your faithless lovers meet,
A hackle raised, a sniff,
Formalities complete, jog on.

Home, lie sunning in the grass;
Heigh ho, for it is spring,
The silly season,
How love can pass.

Boom Boom

Gentlemen poets, so much admired
You've made the cannon

Now – you're fired.

Simple Truth

You die and go
and leave me here
with tears

strange and quite unfair
I absolutely know
it's not just human fear
but bald and naked truth
that never will I hear — exchange
words with you again

there lies the endless silence
and — the human pain.

Death and Sex

Don't say a word

Ah my dear
it is a fact
that death and sex
have a pact

old sex it was
the big taboo
something ladies
did not do – oh no

it just was *not* for you,
but now-a-days
it's all quite changed
relationships are re-arranged
for immediate satisfaction

on the spot
flesh in action – oh hey
in every kind of sexual way
anytime of night or day

a heave a sweat
any juice that you can get,
a suck, a snuggle
a bite, a cock

to give the partner
thrilling shocks
experience orgasms
one two three
that's not learnt

at mother's knee
oh the joy of life to be
free to make it every way
in any kind of sexual play

a groan a moan
a scream   a shout
delicious pleasure
is all about pressing

the right buttons and
bliss is there, with your
partner then to share.
Now, you see, of guilt

we are entirely free –
we've revolutionised
the whole affair – to
have it now without a care –

so on the deepfreeze on the stair –
with anyone you fancy
in a wink panties will be off –
and if you're willing to catch an eye

across a room – no one now
commits to swoon – or blush
or stammer, or be shy for Love
now No One Dares to Die!

But, Time is there and he will come
and he will go, Old Death waits
with him, sure you know, however
much you screw and f..k

Sweet Death will come
to muck it up.

Before All This

Did they have wine
    in the Garden of Eden?
Did they roll out into
    the cold draft of reality
to make it their own
    without interference
from higher powers?

The serpent stayed behind
    to keep God company.
Opposites attract and they
    needed each other to
fulfil their plans.
    So Adam and Eve
increased and multiplied and
    as far as I can see
filled the whole earth.

Earth tries to survive and
    so far hangs on in there
despite the abuses we create
    with the powers that be
with heaven and hell and all of
    us jolly old humankind.

Moon

The night is still.
Moon lies over it.

Its individual light
is all its own, casting
its circle down – a kind of
bright – magic that each
of us can own and bring
into our soul. Lies there

in spacious skies
we dream on it, we fools
with foolish minds. Moon can cast
a sort of spell so we leave
the world behind, give wild
kisses – dare – are quite blind
to bald reality, but what good
does that straight subject give?

Under the moon's light
I learnt to live

A Pure Note

When you feel dark death
creeping near, it's time my love,
to sing to sing not the time
    for prayer

Keeping Mobile

When I die and go below
Please put with me
My mobile phone

Keep it topped up
In case I find
I've had a change of mind.

The End

ANNE LE MARQUAND HARTIGAN is a prize-winning poet, playwright and painter. She trained as a painter at Reading University, England. She returned to Co. Louth, Ireland, in 1962 with her husband Tim Hartigan where they farmed and reared their six children. She now lives in Dublin. She has published six previous collections of poetry: *To Keep The Light Burning: Reflections in times of loss* (Salmon, 2008); *Nourishment* (Salmon, 2005); *Immortal Sins* (Salmon, 1993); the award winning long poem with Anne's drawings, *Now is a Moveable Feast* (Salmon, 1991); *Return Single* (Beaver Row Press, 1986); and *Long Tongue* (Beaver Row Press, 1982). Her prose work includes *Clearing The Space: A Why of Writing* (Salmon, 1996). Her play *Beds* was performed at the Damer Hall in 1982 as part of the Dublin Theatre Festival. Hartigan won the Mobil Prize for Playwriting for her play *The Secret Game* in 1995. *In Other Worlds* (2003) was commissioned and performed by Ohio University, USA, then performed at the Edinburgh Fringe Festival and Otago, Dunedin, New Zealand. *Jersey Lilies* was performed at the Samuel Beckett Theatre, Dublin 1996, where Anne acted with Robert Gordon in this two hander. *La Corbiere* was performed at the Project Theatre during the Dublin Theatre Festival 1989, and has since been performed in Beirut 2004 and by Solas Nua Theatre Company in Washington DC July 2006 where it was the pick of the Fringe festival.

Painting
The author has had many exhibitions of her paintings
and awards for her batik. She has had one-woman and two-person
shows, and major group shows in Ireland and England.